"Every word in this book makes me weep with joy for the God who made the man who went on a long journey to find me, to disciple me, to model for me how to walk 'with him'; for the man who, at 90, went on to write this book. Do you want to know how a Bible-believing Christian can befriend a person like me? If so, then read this book."

Rosaria Butterfield, author of The Secret Thoughts of an Unlikely Convert and Openness Unhindered

"Short yet rich, clear yet profound, demanding yet thrilling, here is a wonderful path into the heart of productive Christian discipleship. We learn how and why the Lord Jesus enriched the men whom he had chosen to serve him, with emphasis especially on the way in which they were trained to be used to bring others into the kingdom. This is presented in the light of today – how we are to dwell close to Christ, praying then to be led to those whom we may help to grow, so that they too may reach out to others. Ken Smith has written these pages after more than half a century of fruitful experience, evidenced in the lives and ministry of many transformed by the Lord through him. May this be used to help equip a new generation of Christian disciples."

Ted Donnelly, professor, author, conference speaker and retired pastor

"Do you want to faithfully follow Jesus? Then sit at the feet of this master disciple-maker to learn the 'with him' principle. I was 'his man' and because of his example the multiplication of men continues."

Vince Ward, Teaching Elder, RPCNA and Missionary Director, Every Village

"Ken Smith raises key points of discipleship that are worth emphasizing. The fact that this is written by an experienced pastor who has been able to put these principles into practice makes this book so valuable."

Derek Leaf, National Ministry Leader for the UK Navigators

WITH HIM

A BIBLICAL MODEL OF DISCIPLESHIP FOR MEN

KEN G. SMITH

a division of 10ofthose.com

First published in Great Britain in 2017. Reprinted once.

British Library Cataloguing in Publication Data

A record for this book is available from the British Library

ISBN: 978-1-911272-34-2
Designed by Diane Warnes
Printed in Denmark by Nørhaven

10Publishing, a division of 10ofthose.com
Unit C Tomlinson Road, Leyland, PR25 2DY, England
Email: info@10ofthose.com
Website: www.10ofthose.com

"THE BRIDGE BUILDER"
BY WILL ALLEN DROMGOOLE

An old man going a lone highway,
Came, at the evening cold and gray,
To a chasm vast and deep and wide.
Through which was flowing a sullen tide
The old man crossed in the twilight dim,
The sullen stream had no fear for him;
But he turned when safe on the other side
And built a bridge to span the tide.

"Old man," said a fellow pilgrim near,
"You are wasting your strength with building here;
Your journey will end with the ending day,
You never again will pass this way;
You've crossed the chasm, deep and wide,
Why build this bridge at evening tide?"

The builder lifted his old gray head;
"Good friend, in the path I have come," he said,
"There followed after me to-day
A youth whose feet must pass this way.
This chasm that has been as naught to me
To that fair-haired youth may a pitfall be;
He, too, must cross in the twilight dim;
Good friend, I am building this bridge for him!"[1]

CONTENTS

NOTE TO THE READER   11

INTRODUCTION   13

THE "WITH HIM" THEORY   17

FINDING THE MEN   27

APPLYING THE "WITH HIM" PRINCIPLE   39

FURTHER REFLECTIONS   59

REFERENCES   63

NOTE TO THE READER

The Bible speaks to us in *principles*. Principles are axioms of truth which have a universal application. So when thinking in terms of Christian *discipleship*, for example, the truth applies to all, men and women. This brief book lays out some of the fundamentals when it comes to helping new believers in Christ. While the accent may seem to fall heavily on men, the principles are usually applicable to both sexes. Such is true about biblical *discipleship*: the principles apply to both.

INTRODUCTION

I was spellbound! As I sat there in First Presbyterian Church in downtown Pittsburgh, I heard a man speaking about multiplying disciples committed to Jesus Christ. I had not heard much about "multiplying" followers of Christ in my seminary training. My denomination had been decreasing in membership as long as I could remember, and my seminary training had virtually omitted any prospects of that changing. But here was hope! Here was a man who not only knew about "discipleship" in Christian terms, but had seen hundreds of servicemen come to Christ as a result of the ministry of one man whom he had trained to reach others, with the new disciples in turn reproducing other new believers (telling the gospel to others), and so on. I was hooked! And I determined to learn everything I could about it. I dogged his steps to hear him while he was in the city, and eventually asked him for help. The man was Dawson Trotman, founder of the Navigators, who helped Billy Graham develop a follow-up plan for his crusades. Dawson died in 1956 at the age of fifty saving a girl from drowning in Schroon Lake,

New York. But his ministry lives on as a result of the men he helped equip and train.

When I went to Dawson for help, I asked him to send us a man to Pittsburgh who could help us learn these principles. As a result LeRoy Eims, a former marine, came to our city. Since I was a single pastor with an empty parsonage, he and his family moved in. I used to say, "He lived in my house; I lived in his family." But the point is I was *with him*. We had two very productive years together. And because I was *with him*, I could both observe and also participate *with him* in his ministry as he reached other men for Christ. As a result the gospel multiplied.

I now understood the very simple principle Jesus practiced during His years on earth. As Mark 3:14–15 says, "And he appointed twelve (whom he also named apostles) so that they might be with him and he might send them out to preach and have authority to cast out demons." It's so simple. He wanted them *with Him*. From these men, except one, He would initiate a world conquest for reaching lost men, women, and children for their eternal salvation and the building of His church and kingdom.

THE "WITH HIM" THEORY

I suppose the idea behind this "with him" practice is so obvious it seems ludicrous to try to spell it out. But the practice is foreign to much, perhaps most, of the church in Western countries. The idea used to be embraced by becoming an "apprentice," but we don't hear that term very often any more, except in industry. It was key in Trotman's thinking. He kept asking, "Where's your man?" In other words, who is the man you're discipling? Whom do you have *with you* whom you are coaching to walk with Christ? And his aggressive probe was not just to pastors, but to anyone who claimed to be a Christian walking with Christ. On more than one occasion he challenged me, "Where's your man? Where are your men?"

For a person who is acquainted with the Bible, this idea should not seem strange. We see it first when Noah was assigned the task of building the ark. He had three sons whom the Bible includes in that great effort. In fact, his sons and their wives were *with Noah* on the ark. It was through them the generations of mankind would in the years to come populate the earth. Hebrews

11:7 shows that Noah's interest was not just in the ark, but in his family: "By faith Noah, being warned by God concerning events as yet unseen, in reverent fear constructed an ark for the saving of his household." His sons were *with him* in that massive construction … which would save their lives. They, with their wives, would now be the ones to multiply and fill the earth.

Later Scripture tells us that Moses had a young man *with him* very early in his experience of leading Israel through the desert, and that young man, Joshua, would actually become Moses' successor and take the nation into the promised land. We see it too in the life of David, who built his army with men who had been *with him* in his earlier escapades with King Saul. It's interesting also to note how Elijah enlisted his "disciple," Elisha. Like the fishermen Jesus would later recruit, Elisha dropped everything and followed his new mentor. And he persisted in being *with him* right up to the time when Elijah was taken up to heaven in a chariot of fire. Thus Elisha became empowered by the Spirit to continue the ministry of Elijah, and Israel was blessed. In short, this concept of mentoring has a long history.

Some years ago I was speaking of this principle with Dr. Elizabeth Coleman, a professor at the University of Pennsylvania in Philadelphia. She mentioned to me that up until 1929 medical schools training physicians always had their students working with corpses. But in that revolutionary year they began taking their students "on the floor" to be dealing with *live* patients. Thus we now see a physician visiting patients with students clustered about him or her, witnessing the events and the conversations. And this "with him/her" practice even accompanies the surgeons into what is known as the operating "theater." It's the experience of being there on site to watch, then later to inquire, learn, and ultimately perform. It makes sense.

Likewise, when I was in high school during the Second World War, I worked in Florida Aircraft in Orlando, Florida, during the summers. My first summer I was assigned to the fabric department where we covered wings. (You need to understand that the Stearman PT-17 was the primary trainer for pilots learning to fly with the Army Air Corps, as it was then called, and it was an open-cockpit bi-plane: a two-seater with wings, tail, and fuselage covered with fabric.) I had to learn from scratch what was involved in this "covering" process, but Mr. Moore, the old-timer there, showed me what was involved, including holding a mouthful of tacks to use with the magnetic hammer. (No, I never swallowed one!) Once the wings were tightly covered and tightly tacked to the inner rib, we coated them five times with clear lacquer in order to make the fabric stronger and airtight, lightly sanding them between each coat. Finally we sent them off to the paint department for the finish color coat. There were many processes involved, but I learned how to do that from the *mentoring* of Mr. Moore and then trying my hand.

This same approach to learning is seen in the term "disciple," as Luke, the gospel writer, spells out in Luke 6:40: "A disciple is not above his teacher, but everyone when he is fully trained will be like his teacher." In short, one can see in people the traits of their teacher. "You sound like …" we say. And so it was that the leaders of the Jews who had crucified Jesus recognized later in His men His characteristics. Luke writes in Acts 4:13, "Now when they saw the boldness of Peter and John, and perceived that they were uneducated, common men, they were astonished. And they recognized that they had been with Jesus." It was their fluency and confidence that struck their listeners. They were *like* Jesus. That is the central focus of the serious Christian: be like Jesus. That is why when Jesus called His men, He did not just say, "Listen to Me …." He said, "Follow me." To do that they had to drop everything and be *with Him*.

An Italian communist produced a film years ago, *The Gospel of Matthew*, which was second rate but very powerful in that he portrayed a purposeful Jesus on the move in mission. The Twelve were pictured as stumbling along behind Him, trying to keep up so they could hear what He was saying. I do not like pictures of Jesus, but I was impressed that this producer, in studying Matthew, had caught the mission aura of Jesus' ministry. To learn from Jesus, of course, you had to *follow Him*. He was on the move. He was obeying His Father in heaven. That's really the posture of a follower of Christ, a true disciple. It's movement! It's kingdom mission! And it is obedience.

Three components make up a true learning situation. First, there is the one who *knows*; second there must be the one who wants to *learn*. Third, there must be the *environment* in which it's learned. It is this final piece that marks Jesus' way to developing His twelve disciples. Of course

Jesus also gave *verbal instruction*. Scripture tells us that Jesus went about all of the area *teaching* His listeners. To take an example, in Matthew 5–7, which has become known as "the Sermon on the Mount," the disciples were there. In fact, there is reason to believe that when Jesus saw the crowds, He intentionally turned and taught His disciples in the context of a listening crowd, because ultimately these disciples would be the men to reach the people.

Jesus did not neglect to instruct His disciples in the truth of the Word of God. But my point is that they learned most of it out in the public arena where Jesus ministered, though at times He would leave the crowds and talk to them privately to make sure they understood. They learned in the *context* of gospel ministry. That experience was going to make a great difference to them as they later were confronted by similar crowds and hostile critics. They'd actually been *with* Jesus as He suffered these things. Consequently they were not caught off guard when later facing the same circumstances.

One of the best examples to me of how to disciple was the late D. James Kennedy of Fort Lauderdale. Yet it is common knowledge among those who knew him that, in his earliest days as a pastor, he was taught how to evangelize by an older pastor in the Carolinas who had invited him to come and preach a series of evangelistic messages. As he told us, "Every afternoon this pastor took me out knocking on doors to invite persons to church and also explain the gospel." But wasn't he the visiting evangelist? Yet here he was learning firsthand from his veteran host how to present the gospel to people! He learned from that out-on-the-street experience. Back in his home church he later developed what became known as "Evangelism Explosion," a way to conduct visitation evangelism for one's church. He also took care to take others *with him* in this task. I have colleagues who had been with him as they knocked on doors there in Fort Lauderdale to follow up visitors at worship, and he maintained that discipline for the rest of his ministry: one night a week visiting with a colleague in the neighborhood. It was a principle he learned not by reading a book, but by a man who took him with him in the actual activity. Likewise, it was a principle he shared *with* others. By now you should have grasped the theory! By being with your mentor *as* he ministers, you learn both how to minister and how to conduct yourself in the process. You also experience the fellowship of the Lord Jesus Himself by His Holy Spirit who is there.

The benefits of this "with him" principle are many: men who accompany their mentor actually *visit* people, learning to make observations in homes, learning how to listen, and so forth. Sometimes it can also reveal a great gap in a learner's grasp of the truth. One night I took a young man from seminary out to visit homes in the neighborhood with a gospel presentation. We had been to Mr. Bucie's place before, and he warmly welcomed us each time we came. We shared *with him* the gospel from John and this night I asked my colleague to lead the conversation. He did a commendable job of it. But then Mr. Bucie asked, "Well, what do I do to get it?" My companion froze. He looked frantically at me, then back to Mr. Bucie, and said, "Well, Mr. Bucie, there's really nothing you can do." The man responded, "Well, it sure sounds great! I just don't know how you get it."

The problem was that my seminary student had come into contact in class with the truth of "total depravity," the impossibility of a sinner doing anything to save himself. Yet what he did not know was how, in that light, to call sinners to real repentance and faith, and therefore he had no real answer for this hungry inquirer. As we returned to the seminary, we had a great opportunity to think through his theology. He then understood the gospel call is based upon God's election and human responsibility. We freely call all men and women to repent and believe the gospel. That night my friend learned theology in the context of sharing the gospel with me, and I was glad the Lord had exposed his need. He learned on site in a way he would never forget. Nor would I. Also, and wonderfully, Mr. Bucie committed his life to Christ.

To summarize, the "with him" principle which Jesus employed in training His men was crucial. It was not unique—the practice of being with one's teacher was seen, for example, in the "pedagogue" in ancient Greece who led his pupil to school. The uniqueness of Jesus' teaching was who He is. As the Son of God Jesus came to redeem His people from sin and its eternal condemnation. He came to "bring us to God ..." (1 Pet. 3:18). He was full of the Spirit and went about doing good. Ultimately He died on the cross and then rose from the dead so that by faith in Him we would be saved from hell and given everlasting life. He trained His men to preach this good news or "gospel." They were witnesses of Jesus' life, death, and resurrection because they had been *with Him*. They had seen it all.

It's a simple concept. From the perspective of Christian discipleship, we do not minister alone. We imitate Jesus and take another or others with us.

FINDING THE MEN

PRAYING FOR MEN

When I have spoken about this matter of training with church leaders, I have often run into the question, "Where do you get such men?" The thought behind the question is that such men just are not available. And indeed that is a real challenge. Remember God's comment in Ezekiel 22:30: "I sought for a man among them who should build up the wall and stand in the breach before me for the land, that I should not destroy it, but I found none."

Without sounding simplistic, let me address this challenge. I noted when I was first exposed to this concept of "training men" for ministry and outreach that Jesus spent the night in prayer before He chose the Twelve. It is therefore no wonder when He looked on the crowds as scattered sheep wandering and without food, direction, or leadership that He told His men, "The harvest is plentiful, but the laborers are few; therefore pray earnestly to the Lord of the harvest to send out laborers into his harvest" (Matt. 9:37–38). Don't miss this: Jesus taught His men to look to God for such workers. Doesn't that mean that God will raise up such men as we ask Him for them?

This approach to the problem is confirmed in John 17:6, Jesus' intercessory prayer to the Father for His men, where He identified those men as "the people whom you gave me out of the world ...." I gather from this that the men we seek are men who already have some sense of hunger or call from God to grow and reach others. Those men are just waiting for someone to encourage them to rise to this challenge.

Therefore, when I've been asked, "Where do you get these men?" I have simply said, "On my knees. Then I watch for them." Wherever I have been, I have found certain men ready to alter their schedules to learn how to walk with Christ and reach out to other men. But I have "discovered" them through private conversation. They had been waiting until then for a challenge that had never come. They were ready now for a manly challenge that demanded their life.

COMING ALONGSIDE MEN

There is another problem though. In our churches there seem to be many a "Joe Christian," a guy seeming to be something less than a spiritually minded, aggressive witness for the Lord Jesus—

and a congregation that appears happy to have it so. As I have pondered this, I have been reminded of something Dwight Eisenhower (whose military career included him being Commander-in-Chief of the Allied Forces) wrote about the early days of the Second World War and the condition of American troops. General McNair had taken his men out on maneuvers. When he returned, he reported to Eisenhower that the troops were terribly undisciplined; however, he contended they were capable of the best discipline. To this Eisenhower issued the following announcement: "Where troops are undisciplined, leadership will be replaced." It was in that mode the United States military became equipped for armed battles to follow. Likewise church leaders need to be proactive in instilling spiritual action in the lives of their church members.

This need is something that Richard Halverson, then pastor of Hollywood Presbyterian Church and later the Chaplain of the United States Senate, learned from an experience with one of the men in his church. In the course of conversation over lunch the man began to weep. Halverson was startled and asked if he had said something wrong. "O no," the man said, "I just didn't think you pastors had time for men like us." Shocked, Halverson was jolted. As a result he changed his whole approach to his ministry. From then on, he gave his best attention to *men*. He later sent out a regular letter—afterward compiled into a book[2] —to encourage them in their Christian walk. My experience in my denomination supported this view of the general condition in our churches. Men as men were just not the focus of pastors. (Of course women too need to be discipled. Those who perform this role—whether as women's workers or as older women in the church—are to be greatly valued.)

When on occasion I have preached just to the men in the congregation, the response of the women has been interesting. For example, one time in the suburbs of Ottawa, Ontario, I told the congregation in the morning service that I wanted all the men to be present that evening and I would be preaching only to men. To this the women all smiled approvingly and some spoke to me appreciatively. I'm sure they understood, as I am persuaded, that there is a deep emptiness in many men in our churches. They personally have never experienced man-to-man discipleship. They may even be unsure of their salvation. The writer to the Hebrews, in 5:12, encountered the same problem: "For though by this time you ought to be teachers, you need someone to teach you again the basic principles of the oracles of God. You need milk, not solid food ...."

As was Halverson's experience, however, many men feel that their pastor has no time for them personally. Their pastor's vision does not seem to include this perspective of training the men in their churches to mature and become skilled in reaching others for Christ. So while the men of many churches may appear disinterested and unavailable, leaders must first spend time with them alone and inquire of their Christian faith and service

Dawson Trotman, when in the early days of his Christian experience, taught a class of young boys. On a particular occasion, one of them had really disrupted the class and Trotman asked him to stay after the others had left. He told the boy he had been acting like a devil! Then he challenged him next week to act like an angel. As he told this story to us, he chuckled and commented: "Boys lose their stinger when you get them alone." I later picked up on that and concluded that men are just big boys. You need to get them alone and then really get to know them.

COMBATTING OUR CULTURE

Our prevailing culture makes the problem of finding available men even worse. My wife and I served some time in a suburb of Melbourne, Australia. While there I wanted to understand better Australian men. So I ventured into a shop and engaged the proprietor in friendly chat. He could tell by my speech I was American. "Tell me about Australian men," I probed. He spoke openly and freely explaining they were genuine, helpful, friendly, and so forth. I then asked, "What about religion?" His two hands went up objecting. "It's not discussed," he said. "That's a closed topic." I found out he was right. Sunday in Melbourne is all about football. There were two boys in our Sunday school in Melbourne—there without their father. Once they became sixteen, we never saw them again. Their dad had influence over their priorities and it was football that had become their focus. As a result he had cut off our contact with his boys. The culture had won. We were stymied by it and realized again that culture wars against us, seducing men with all kinds of idols and distracting them from what is crucial. We're in a life-and-death conflict—make no mistake about it.

Yet the man is the key to the family in that God's plan is for the father to take the initiative in rearing the children. Some men realize this and take their responsibility seriously. For example, some men in Cincinnati, Ohio, had a group called "For Fathers Who Aren't in Heaven." They met each week to encourage one another in the Lord. They gathered at an early hour, like 6 a.m., so that it worked without conflicting with their other schedules. They considered this time a priority and didn't miss it. As a result, their lives began to change. As one women commented to a visitor at their church, who inquired about the group, "That's the most important gathering of the week in this church." Christ-centered fellowship plays a big role in leading men—just as Jesus Himself had twelve male disciples.

Our challenge to reach men is not simple. Man is a fallen creature who is full of pride. He's locked up inside and—he thinks—holds the key to his future. But he's wrong! God holds the key, and unless He shows mercy to this stubborn heart, man will plunge to his eternal death and perish in hell. So men need to hear the gospel. If a man repents and comes to Christ, he will be saved; but then he will need plenty of personal help to learn how to follow His new Savior and Lord. This is where pastors and mature men of the church should be there to help him.

THE NEED TO TRAIN PASTORS THEMSELVES IN DISCIPLESHIP

A problem arises, however, if such mature Christian men—who would be in a position to disciple others—are missing. And if the men of our church are *undiscipled* (rather than *undisciplined*), should we employ Eisenhower's principle that the leadership needs to be replaced? It's not quite that simple. What if pastors have never themselves been personally discipled? What if no one ever shepherded them to learn to walk with Christ? What if that side of ministry was omitted from their seminary experience? In most cases I would maintain that the church leadership has not itself been trained to nurture and equip men as men. Indeed, there has been a "feminization of Western culture," about which sociologists, including women, have written.

As a result of their lack of experience and training, there is a tendency for many ministers in practice simply to say, "Listen to me, and you will catch on." I was that way. Having been taught something about how to preach, I preached. How to respond to my teaching I considered the congregation's challenge. But conceiving they might need personal help if they would ever become able to reach others with the gospel was not in my mind. I did not have this vision, let alone any inclination of how to do so.

I remember sitting in the study of a pastor out in the Midwest, during the time I was serving as Christian Education Director. We had been discussing the role of men in the church and its importance. He began to weep. I hesitated. Had I said something amiss? He quickly assured me the reason was not me, but his own awareness of his lack. He asked, "Ken, what do you do with those men you have in training? What do you say to them?" I felt his frustration. He had no concept whatever of developing other men to "minister" so the gospel could multiply.

Historically, teaching about the pastor's role has reinforced this way of thinking. In Ephesians 4:11–12, the King James Bible reads, "And he gave some, apostles; and some, prophets; and some, evangelists; and some, pastors and teachers; For the perfecting of the saints, for the work of the ministry, for the edifying of the body of Christ …." Matthew Henry, a respected pastor in the seventeenth and eighteenth century, explained this passage in his popular commentary[3] by stating that these three instructions outline a pastor's job description: 1. perfecting the saints (that is, believers); 2. the work of ministry; and 3. the building up of the saints (believers) in their faith. This meant the term "ministry," as it had become commonly used, was seen to apply to the pastor alone. He was *the* minister. Certainly my training in seminary fitted this historic model.

But modern translations have caught the more accurate rendition. Instead of seeing these as three dimensions of the pastor's agenda, they are rather linked together as progressive aspects of one task, namely, as the ESV renders it, "... to equip the saints for the work of ministry, for building up of the body of Christ ..." (v. 12). In other words, the pastor's task is to "equip" or train the members to serve or minister themselves so the church is built up. Ephesians 4:16 adds that it is "when each part is working properly" that the whole body of Christ grows "so that it builds itself up in love." Every member is to be built up to fulfill his or her function in the body, the church. And the focus of the pastor's work is to help each person find his or her place of service within the community of believers.

I sympathize with pastors who have no understanding of ministry to men. If they had been trained to fulfill the three roles Matthew Henry outlines, omitting the aspect of equipping believers to minister, then there is little reason for them to be blamed. They were not trained to teach others to minister. I understand that deficiency from firsthand experience—I was not trained in seminary with such a vision for my future work in mind; I acquired it from another source. Yet the result is a dilemma: men who seem unavailable for training in discipleship on the one hand and pastors who lack either the vision or the know-how in training other men on the other hand.

Often this seeming roadblock is overcome through developing men's fellowship groups. Men like comradery. It's in groups like these that conversations often open up in which men feel free to discuss their desires and hopes. It's catalytic. Though often men are slower than women to open up to one another, they will in genuine *fellowship*. And it's there they often sense another's need and step in to help.

Happily there are many men who have been called by God—not only pastors but other men of

God—who are in the context of their ordinary life "disciple makers." These men have learned how to walk with Jesus and obey His will, and they reach out to other men and equip them to train still others. The result is a *multiplication* of new disciples. When I understood the importance and significance of this discipling process, I became an excited pastor!

APPLYING THE
"WITH HIM" PRINCIPLE

When Jesus called the Twelve to be *with Him*, His purpose was to train and equip them so they could fulfill His purpose to spread the gospel to the world, though it was true that these men were special—they would become the apostles who would be used of God to bring about the establishing and growth of His church. When the New Testament speaks about the "apostles' teaching" in Acts 2:42, it is referring to the truth Jesus taught His men and on which Christ's church would be built. That is the truth contained in the Bible, and, as 2 Timothy 3:16 says, "All Scripture is … profitable for teaching." In the same way for us biblical discipleship assumes coming to know biblical doctrine. This is the "what" of discipleship, which underlies the "how."

In one sense, this "with him" principle is a very small truth. I don't want to exaggerate it, because in many ways it's just common sense. However, having said that, it is still an essential truth. When I was at seminary, I remember our professor one day asked us, "What is the most important part of the ignition system on your car?" No part is more important than any other, so his point was simply this: it takes *every* part functioning to make the ignition system work. It's a "system."

I see this "with him" principle as being a very small aspect of the big biblical system, but it's a vital one. It's part of the system. And because of its neglect, there are many churches that today treasure the truth of the historical gospel, but yet are dying. To neglect this idea of training men in the gospel is enough to severely cripple, and even stop the spread of the gospel. The system halts. Think of the same principle but within a family context. How well fathers, and mothers, are instructing their children matters. If the "with him or her" principle is missing in the home and the children are not being nurtured in all aspects of their development, this certainly has a negative impact on them. I hope you are now convinced of how important the same principle is to your church.

We have established the significance of the concept. Let's follow this through by looking at how it works.

DISCIPLESHIP INVOLVES TEACHING GOD'S TRUTH

I think the vision of men with us in the work of ministry is probably best summarized in 2 Timothy 2:2. The apostle Paul is writing to a man, Timothy, he himself had trained in gospel ministry and who is now out on his own. So his mentor writes, "… what you have heard from me in the presence of many witnesses entrust to faithful men, who will be able to teach others also." Notice that there are four "generations" of men involved in this work of discipleship: Paul to Timothy to "faithful men" to "others". If we have such a vision, we can expect our ministry to multiply. But it means we must also have an eye out for men, whom God has prepared, who are available and spiritually hungry for discipleship. We must think this way, with this perspective. We should always be looking for disciples!

Let's look at the example of Paul in more detail to understand exactly what such discipleship will involve. Paul had received some help upon his conversion to Christ from a man from Cyprus named Barnabas. Barnabas was known for his patient spirit and it was he who took Paul under his wing, so to speak, until he became oriented to being a Christian. Paul also had such a dangerous reputation among Christians, because of his previous persecution of them, that it took Barnabas some time to convince them his conversion to Christ was for real (Acts 9:26–27). So from Barnabas Paul learned the principle of discipleship, and now he in turn enlists Timothy to be *with him*. When Paul finds Timothy in Asia Minor (today's Turkey), he is already a believer in Christ. Paul first checks his reputation (Acts 16:1–2) and then takes Timothy to accompany him as he ventures out to city after city to spread the gospel. Thus this whole "multiplication of men" process is implemented.

Paul is quite conscious of what Timothy learns from him: "... what you have heard from me in the presence of many witnesses ...." (2 Tim. 2:2). It is clear from this that having a man, or men, with you is more than just fellowship, though this is part of the picture. Instead it's like going out together into battle, in the course of which much can be learned from observation. In 2 Timothy 3:10–11 Paul reviews all that Timothy has absorbed from him and it reads like a catalogue of courses available in some learning institute: "You, however, have followed my teaching, my conduct, my aim in life, my faith, my patience, my love, my steadfastness ...." Paul seems to know what he had in his life that was valuable for Timothy to learn. While it is not my purpose here to analyze each of these items, do pay attention to them.

In a similar way, when our boys were still at home and growing up, I used to drill them on the fact that they would be going into a world that was hostile intellectually to all Christians, and they should be prepared for this. I taught them that as Christians they would confront three basic questions: "what is true?;" "what is valuable?;" and "what is ethical?" I instructed them that their answers, as followers of Jesus, should be: the Word of God is truth; the kingdom of God is valuable; and the law of God is ethical. They are now grown men with families but they have not forgotten my training.

Do not miss this key point that the first "course" listed in Paul's mentoring plan is *teaching*, or what I might label as true doctrine. Moreover, the emphasis is how important it is that a man think *according to Scripture*. Paul makes this point in 2 Timothy 3:16: "All Scripture is breathed out by God and profitable for teaching, for reproof, for correction, and for training in righteousness."

All the time the Twelve were with Jesus they were learning how to think and act biblically. They heard Him and they watched Him. For example, they heard Him challenge the Scribes' and Pharisees' mishandling of the Old Testament. They also observed that He spoke with the sick and hurting, and was comfortable talking with women and holding their children.

The beauty and fun of having men with you as you minister to others is that all kinds of questions arise naturally. That is why, as I mentioned earlier, medical students now shadow a physician while learning their skills. So too Paul follows the same tradition and makes sure Timothy has grasped the true doctrine of the gospel. That is fundamental. Being with Paul in all his experiences is Timothy's classroom.

To summarize this first step, it's evident that the apostle Paul was actively reminding Timothy of all that he'd learned so he could pass it along to other men. We see this in 2 Timothy 4:1-2, where Paul writes, "I charge you in the presence of God and of Christ Jesus ...: preach the word; be ready in season and out of season; reprove, rebuke, and exhort, with complete patience and teaching." We've already seen that those men were to share the same training to yet others, and so forth, thus leading to a multiplication of men equipped for Christian service. Don't lose sight of this vision and the "with him" principle that drives it.

DISCIPLESHIP INVOLVES LIVING BY FAITHFUL EXAMPLE

If we return to Paul's reminder to Timothy in 2 Timothy 2:2, we see that he advocates the need for "faithful men, who will be able to teach others also." The men Paul challenges Timothy to teach are to be *faithful*. It is therefore vital to ask yourself whether you are a *faithful* man. Can you be trusted?

This need for faithfulness is illustrated by an incident that my friend LeRoy Eims told me. As a Navigator staff member, he was visiting a well-known military school where they had some contacts, because he wanted to see how these men were getting along. So he knocked on their door. They were both surprised and astounded! The renowned LeRoy Eims of the Navigators was standing in front of them! Then LeRoy saw their room: Beds unmade; dirty clothes on the floor; wastebaskets running over …. As LeRoy studied the scene and told them it was a total mess, the men began to apologize. They tried to come up with one excuse or another. Finally they said, "We're just undisciplined."

At this point LeRoy objected. He said, "What do you mean you're undisciplined? You are among the elite of the military, the most disciplined of all men! No, you're disciplined; you're just not *faithful*." His message was clear: you must live in the light of who you claim to be.

Jesus emphasized the necessity of being faithful to Him. When He called men to follow Him, He said, "If anyone would come after me, let him deny himself and take up his cross daily and follow me" (Luke 9:23). As we know, one of the Twelve defected; Judas was not faithful. Yet while the other eleven had much to learn and made plenty of mistakes, they were after all faithful men. We see this same faithfulness in John 6. Many people who had been following Christ began to bail out when His revelation of His doctrine became too tough for them to contemplate. In verse 60 they proclaim, "This is a hard saying; who can listen to it?" Therefore, as verse 66 recounts, "After this many of his disciples turned back and no longer walked with him." So Jesus then turns to His disciples and asks, "Do you want to go?" (v. 67). If they wanted it, there was their chance! There was an open door to go back to their old way of life, with no questions asked. But Peter's response is that of a *faithful* man: "Lord, to whom shall we go? You have the words of eternal life ...." (v. 68). A faithful man in terms of the Christian faith is a man who is totally committed to follow Christ's call on his life for as long as he lives.

Therefore if you expect to be someone who trains others, you must *be* what you want other men to *become*. I'm sure there are many men who have an undisciplined and unfaithful walk with Christ and yet blame others or their circumstances for this. Men who are hungry for spiritual training will always discern whether their mentor is faking it or for real. So, if you are going to be a man who can train others to follow Christ, and who will minister for Him in other men's lives, you must yourself be an example of how to do that. And by the power and blessing of the Holy Spirit, you can be that kind of man. But you must become serious about your own Christian life, for example getting rid of the idols in your life. The apostle Paul was such a mentor, and therefore could write to the Philippians, "What you have learned and received and heard and seen in me—practice these things, and the God of peace will be with you" (Phil. 4:9).

Men also need to see from you that true Christian obedience costs your life: it involves suffering as a follower of Christ. We see this vividly in the example of Paul. He has given Timothy full-blown exposure to many areas of development, but in addition Timothy gains a vital education from witnessing the many afflictions Paul experienced in life. As Paul adds in 2 Timothy 3:11: "[You ... have followed] my persecutions and sufferings that happened to me at Antioch, at Iconium, and at Lystra—which persecutions I endured ...." Paul's sufferings involved at times even threats of being thrown to the lions, a favorite sport of some contemporary cities where he had preached (see 2 Timothy 4:14–18).

Dietrich Bonhoeffer, the German Lutheran pastor, wrote of this same cost of following Christ: "When Christ bids a man come and follow Him, He bids him come and die."[4] Bonhoeffer then paid the supreme cost for his faithful walk with Christ: with his life. Having fearlessly spoken out against the Nazi regime, he was executed by them in 1945.

I have never heard of a course in seminary entitled "Persecution." There's a good reason for this: it can't be taught in a classroom! One exception to that could be Christians in a hostile university class under a professor who likes to take Christians apart intellectually. That pressure is real. It is not so much the arguments themselves but often the peer ridicule that gets under one's skin. Yet by adopting a "with him" approach to discipleship, this will expose learners to their mentor's life and ministry. As men who are being discipled witness such pressure firsthand, this helps to mature them to be ready themselves for the battle.

DISCIPLESHIP INVOLVES FRIENDSHIP

I really enjoy reading chapters 13–16 of John's Gospel. It's all about Jesus' time with His men just before He went to the cross. What I find so refreshing and enjoyable is the fellowship I sense between Jesus and His men. Jesus really reveals their pride when He washes their feet. Why had not one of them thought of showing such love to Him? He exposes the counterfeit Judas in the context of instituting the Lord's Supper. Then in 15:15 Jesus calls His men "friends" because He has shared with them everything He has heard from His Father. What an open Mentor these men had! Jesus kept no secrets. He had no hidden agendas. He had spared nothing from them in His openness. What a relationship!

Likewise, if we are to engage in healthy "with him" relationships, we need to exhibit this same true bond of friendship. Our relationships with those we mentor are to have this horizontal dimension, not just the vertical aspect of our teaching them.

For this reason when LeRoy and I lived together on Northside Pittsburgh, we frequently had what he called "Whingdings." These were when we kept an open house for fun! He and I planned these nights very carefully; they had a "flow" to them. Once everyone was there, it was game time—not board games, but group activities. Some nights we had "wall-to-wall" people, so the fun would involve skits staged by the folks themselves. Later, before enjoying refreshments, we had a testimony or brief word from the Scriptures. The fun was clean, creative, and casual! It was one way to exhibit that the Christian life is enjoyable, and as a result friendships were born and deepened.

Such camaraderie is an often neglected aspect of Christian community. Have you ever thought of Jesus just enjoying being with His men? John gives us a glimpse of this. I believe much of that kind of fellowship takes place around the dining table in one's home.

THE PRACTICE OF MAKING DISCIPLES

As with many things we learn, it has to come with practice, not just with understanding the principles. We call it inductive learning rather than deductive learning. In other words it's like swimming. One can read a book about swimming—its great champions and the various strokes and techniques. One could even then pass a written test with all this knowledge. But without practice you still have a problem: you can't swim.

The same thing might be said about discipleship. One may read and study all about it, but until you are actually caught up in being a disciple and learning to follow Christ, you will only know about it. Similarly, without practice it is impossible to be a mature "reproducer of reproducers," to use a Navigators' term.

I suggest that there are six steps involved in making disciples.

1. Have a clear *goal*

When helping a man to learn to walk with the Savior, I envision what by the grace of God he can become. He is to be a man of some measure of maturity. Hebrews 5:12–14 is helpful here. The writer of Hebrews is decrying the fact that, in the time that has gone by since the Jews he is addressing became Christians, they are still needing "milk, not solid food" (v. 12). In short they had not grown spiritually. Then he sets out his goal: "… solid food is for the mature, for those who have their powers of discernment trained by constant practice to distinguish good from evil" (v. 14). In other words we help men become mature in Christ so that they know how to make decisions on the basis of the Word of God. They learn that by practice. It takes a while, but the goal is clear. To this we need to add Jesus' goal for His men: to equip them to preach the gospel and "make disciples of all nations" (Matt. 28:19).

2. Teach a man how to *feed himself* on the Word of God

It is crucial for someone we are discipling to know how to gain the spiritual food that he needs from God's Word. While I was in seminary I learned something of Hebrew, so that I could get into the substance of the Old Testament, and more of Greek, in order to discern the precise meaning of the New Testament. However, I have no recollection of having been taught how to *feed myself* on the Scriptures. What an oversight! In contrast, sometime after that I was at a conference in the St. Bernardino Mountains in California and heard Dr. Howard Hendricks of Dallas Seminary say that when men arrived for three years of study at their seminary, the first year was given to teaching men how to *feed themselves* on the Word of God. I liked that! The steps that follow will expand on how this is done.

Another important aspect of learning to hear, read, study, and memorize the Scripture is very subtle, but crucial to growth. One must approach the Scripture as the Word Himself speaking. In other words it's fellowship with God Himself, not just a book about God. This comes by way of the Spirit drawing us into union and communion with the Lord Jesus Himself. To put it another way, it's communication with God, not just information about God. Therefore when I meet with my "disciple," I share with him what I have found in the Word for *my* life. The next time we meet, I have him share with me what the Lord showed *him*. That's a principle he'll carry with him as long as he lives. He's in union with Christ, and Christ instructs us in the Word of God. Encourage your "disciple" to meet the Lord as he looks at God's Word, not just make Bible reading a habit.

3. Help him to learn to *pray*

Part of enjoying fellowship with God is of course talking to God in prayer. Your "disciple" may not know how to verbalize a prayer, but this is a process that can be learned, just like the way children learn to talk. If they are embarrassed, let them pray silently at first. Later, after hearing others pray out loud, they will begin to do so themselves. As far as what to pray for, lead them step by step through the Lord's Prayer, which Jesus used to teach His disciples to pray.

When I was learning from LeRoy Eims, we used to go to Observation Hill in Riverview Park when we wanted to pray together. One time we prayed about his car, an old Chevy on its last wheels, and prayed for a car for him. The next day the car quit. He was ecstatic: "The Lord's beginning to answer our prayer!" That coming Sunday he spoke to an adult class at church and in passing mentioned the "dead" car. When he finished, a businessman spoke up and said he had a car for him, which then led the class to take up an offering for gasoline! Of course prayer doesn't always happen like that, but it's seeing such answers that motivates a new believer to bring his requests before God.

4. Lead him to learn to *obey* the Scriptures

If your "disciple" is reading the Word, he will come to portions that call for a response, for example a change in his thinking or behavior. Teach him how to respond rightly. One means that has helped many learn to "be doers of the word, and not hearers only" (Jas. 1:22) is known as "ABCD" study. In this plan, as you study a particular portion of the Bible, "A" stands for an *analysis* or outline of the passage. "B" calls for what you would identify as the *basic* or key verse(s) in the section studied. "C" is the life-changing part: your *commitment*, or in other words the application to you of the passage. This "C" stage involves three steps: 1. what truth has God impressed on you in this Scripture? 2. How have you been failing to believe or do what this word says? Perhaps you can try to give an example. 3. Commit yourself to one thing you will do about this. By following this process you take heed of the advice in Psalm 119:59: "When I think on my ways, I turn my feet to your testimonies." The "D" part is for *difficulties*. Write down what you don't understand. What question(s) do you have about the passage? These can be reviewed if in a group study, or can be researched later.

When you teach someone how to respond in this way, have him share what he has written down. And if you're doing the study together, which is a good practice, take time to tell each other what you have jotted down. Then pray for one another to be obedient to your commitment. This type of study can also be very useful in a group study, not just on a man-to-man basis. Remember, though, that the point of it all is to help one another be obedient to the Word. The Lord wants and blesses obedience.

I was part of a group some years ago that met in Belfast, Northern Ireland. One of the young men in the group liked to talk and could ad lib—he was a barrister in training. Yet he would always hold his Bible up in such a way we could not see his written notes from preparing the study. Recognizing that he seemed to be faking his response, I asked him just to read what he had written down. He admitted he had not put anything down on paper. I therefore said, "From now on if you don't get the study completed and written down, you may not speak during the discussion; but you're welcome to listen." This challenge worked: from then on he looked at and wrote down his study beforehand, which meant that he thought carefully about how he needed to obey God's Word.

5. Show him that he needs contact with Christ's people through *church*.

It might be that your "disciple" has never been baptized. If that is the case, encourage him to do so by approaching his church. It is right to make a public declaration that he has committed his life to belong to Jesus Christ as his Lord and Savior. He then needs to be "plugged in" to a church where he can learn to worship with the people of God, to sit under regular Bible teaching from those gifted in this area, and to serve others in whatever ways he can. Being part of a biblical church is God's plan for us all.

Someone unacquainted with the things of the Lord learns *fellowship* in a small group of men who are committed to helping each other grow in the Lord. Though Jesus' disciples were *with Him*, at the same time they were *with one another*. The importance of this dimension of the Christian's life can be seen by observing the many times the phrase "one another" appears in the New Testament. The Christian walk is easiest when it is lived together with other believers rather than alone, as Hebrews

10:24–25 testifies. Therefore make sure your "disciple" is included in such a group.

6. Urge him to preach the gospel to all nations

This is a key command for all Christians. It is for this role that Jesus trained His apostles and hence His church. As their Mentor, Jesus took them *with Him* as He went from town to town proclaiming God's message. We are to follow His model and train others by taking them with us when we share the gospel with unbelievers. Your "disciple" will learn evangelism by this simple exposure, and because it is so easily learned, he in turn can teach others how to do so. If he is faithful, he will. Thus the making of disciples multiplies.

FURTHER REFLECTIONS

One of the most enjoyable and satisfying approaches to this type of man-to-man, or woman-to-woman, training is that which takes place in the home. My wife Floy and I are from large families, so we knew from the start what it was to have folks for dinner. But we also had lived with those from whom we were to learn many of the aspects of discipleship, or the "with him" principle, and thus have sought to share the Christian life in the same way with others. For example, when Floy's sister Lyn was graduated from high school in Arkansas and came to Pittsburgh looking for work before going to college, she lived with us. So did a nurse who became employed at a nearby hospital. My younger brother also spent time in our home. In fact, over the years many have passed through our door who had a longing to know how a Christian home functioned. Together with our eventual three boys, they caught the aura of what Christian home life, family worship, good conversation, the discipline of children, keeping the Lord's Day, and so forth is like in practice. We look back on it now as a very enjoyable part of our life, and all those "observers" became our friends.

It is also a delight to anticipate the eternal status of all true believers in Christ. In heaven we will be *with Him*, our Lord Jesus, in the fellowship of the Father and Holy Spirit. Jesus, after giving His men what we call the "Great Commission," ended His challenge with these words: "And behold, I am with you always, to the end of the age" (Matt. 28:20). While we are not all "apostles," we do all share in that promise. His commitment to be with us who know Him stands forever. So it makes sense that we learn now what it means to be *with Him*! As Psalm 23 expresses it, "Surely goodness and mercy shall follow me all the days of my life, and I shall dwell in the house of the LORD forever."

REFERENCES

1 This poem was possibly first published in 1900.

2 Richard C. Halversone, *Man to Man: Thought-provoking meditations for men* (Zondervan, 1968).

3 Matthew Henry, *Complete Commentary*, now available online.

4 Dietrich Bonhoeffer, *The Cost of Discipleship* (first published 1937).

a division of 10ofthose.com

10Publishing is the publishing house of **10ofThose**.
It is committed to producing quality Christian
resources that are biblical and accessible.

www.10ofthose.com is our online retail arm selling
thousands of quality books at discounted prices.

For information contact: **sales@10ofthose.com**
or check out our website: **www.10ofthose.com**